First published by Rosie Shilo, 2019

© Rosie Shilo 2019

www.virtuallyyours.com.au

Title: The Outsourcing Secret: A stress-free guide to growing your business / Rosie Shilo.

ISBN: 978-0-6484135-1-6 (paperback)

Book cover design and layout by eMatti

Printed and distributed in Australia by IngramSpark

Keywords:
> Outsourcing
> Scaling
> Business growth
> Virtual Assistant
> VA
> Virtually Yours
> Rosie Shilo
> Virtual network

DISCLAIMER

The Outsourcing
Secret

A stress-free guide to
growing your business

ROSIE SHILO
Founder of the Virtually Yours
Virtual Assistant & Training Network

Contents

FOREWORD

by Renée Hasseldine

Best-Selling Author, Speaker,
Podcast Host & Signature System Super Star

shareyourpassion.com.au

MY MISSION IN MY BUSINESS as in life, is to just be me and do what I love. And to empower others to do the same.

A massive key to making this a reality is outsourcing. And when it comes to outsourcing, Rosie Shilo is my 'go to' expert. I'm so excited that she's finally written this book so that I can give a copy to all my clients and business besties. Because I know the pain of outsourcing the 'wrong way'.

It pays to get it right.

So, if you're ready to get it right, you've made a smart move in reading this book, because Rosie knows her stuff.

I work during school hours during school terms, earning multiple six figures, which is more than enough for my little family's lifestyle. My husband's a high school teacher and our two children are in primary school. This means that for 12 weeks a year, during school holidays, we get quality family time.

This is so much more important to me than hustling.

But to think that there's a trade-off between time and money would be wrong. Paying people to do stuff that I don't want to do in my business gives me more time AND more money. Because every time I bring on a new team member, my business grows. There really isn't a down side.

I focus on my zone of genius in my business and I engage team members who work in their respective zones of genius. That is, people who will do their jobs better than I ever would.

I have five virtual assistants on my team: Stevie, Neha, Sol, Mel and Kym. Sol is in the Philippines and the rest are Australian based.

Stevie is my General Manager. She's been with me for more than three years and was my first real outsourcing success. The day Stevie joined the team was a massive turning point for my business. She started out as my content manager, producing weekly blogs, social media posts and newsletters. Suddenly my business had a consistent content marketing strategy and my following began to grow, while I had more time to focus on the billable activities. Now Stevie is my 2IC. She knows the business as well as I do, wrangles me and co-facilitates events. Her role grows as my business does and my life is better with her in it.

Neha is my accountant. Her team also takes care of the book-keeping. Because even though I did accounting and finance at university, I would rather scratch my eyeballs out than deal with that. It's not a good use of my time or energy.

Sol takes care of all the repetitive recurring tasks that need to be done to keep the business running like a well-oiled machine. She takes great joy in making our lives easier, doing what Rosie calls 'LSTs – Life Sapping Tasks'. Training Sol has mostly been done by Stevie. Each new task that is introduced, Stevie records a video of it being done, so that Sol knows exactly what to do. So, as Rosie talks about in the book, you don't need to have all your systems documented before you start. High quality VAs will create them with or even for you!

Mel is our graphic designer. She creates all the sexy models for my clients' Signature Systems. Mel's role is more 'seasonal'. Four times a year, we run our Authority Accelerator program where we extract 4 visual models for 10 clients in 2 days. Mel then does all the graphic design for those 40 models, plus creates the slides, social media images, videos and worksheets for the client. It's intense work for a few weeks for Mel and then it's mostly quiet in between, with the exception of some smaller graphic design tasks we need internally.

Kym is my Executive Assistant and the newest addition to our team. Of course, recruiting Kym was a dream, because I followed Rosie's ABC of Recruitment. Less than a week later, Kym was sorting out my inbox. Kym continues to give me back time, head space and energy by keeping my inbox at zero, managing my calendar, booking travel and event venues. Most importantly, she's adding value to my clients and therefore my business, by taking care of customer service.

Except when I'm running events (and we do run a lot), I work from home. And each team member works from theirs. Having a remote team is a freaking fabulous way to keep business overheads low. I don't have to pay for business premises and all the furniture, IT and other office equipment that involves.

Instead, each team member is paid for the results they deliver in my business. When and where they do that is up to them. With the exception of Sol, who works in my business full-time, my team all run their own businesses. I am one of their clients, but they all make me feel like I'm their highest priority (as I'm sure they do for all their clients).

Even though they are remote and I am their client, that doesn't diminish the need for leadership and team management. I believe in creating a team culture where every team member feels valued, respected and enjoys their work. It's a work in progress, but it's something I will always strive for, because I could not do what I do without my team and I care about them as humans.

We use Slack for ongoing communication throughout the working week, we have weekly team meetings on Zoom and my General Manager, Stevie, and I have monthly strategy days. We have recently introduced quarterly 1:1 check-ins with me and professional development budgets for each team member. This feeds into my mission of ensuring that my team also love what they do.

It feels like I'm finally 'adulting' as a business owner.

Outsourcing to other business owners, means that I have my own permanent mastermind group! Having my team holds me to a higher standard. If I screw up, I'm not just letting myself down, I'm letting them down too. So I am more motivated to be the best version of myself in my business, for all of us. As we grow the business together, I can reward and pay them more.

But this is my eighteenth year in business and up until I got Stevie on board, I was doing business the hard way. I really was a bit late to the party.

If I could go back and give myself some advice, it would be this "OUTSOURCE EARLIER!"

Once you're determined to actually grow your business and work smarter, not harder, then outsourcing is the obvious choice. And if you're ready to outsource, this book is a great place to start.

My advice to you now is simple. Read this book from cover to cover and have a pen and paper handy. You're going to want to take notes. But even more important than taking notes, is taking action.

I know that outsourcing can bring up a whole lot of fear and uncertainty. It's easy to delay it. I did for years, but I wish I didn't. If only I'd had Rosie's step-by-step process, I could have grown so much faster.

So take a deep breath and just do it.

Start outsourcing and do it right.

It's an investment of time and money. For sure.

But when you realise the return on investment, you'll wish you got started sooner. Like me!

The more you outsource, the more time, energy and head space you will have to do what matters.

The results will blow your mind and your family will love you for it.

It really is a no-brainer. So what are you waiting for?

READ ON SUPER STAR!

PREFACE

Working with Contractors

RUNNING A BUSINESS is a special and unique journey. It has massive highs and massive lows. For many, it's a solo journey; working by themselves most of the time, doing all activities from sales, bookkeeping, admin and the actual business activity itself. It can be long hours with very little reward.

Often people start their businesses so they can have more control over their lives. More choice. They want to decide who they work for and when. They want to set their own rates, take holidays and see the kids growing up.

But all too often, business owners find themselves doing the opposite of what they'd set out to do. They start working with anyone who comes along, compromising on their pricing, working long hours, never taking holidays and generally feeling trapped by the 'freedom machine' they'd created.

For some, the thought of running a business may sound very dry and formal, but when it's yours, it's personal. It's something very special to you, and it can be hard to let other people in to help. Especially when you aren't making money like you think you 'should' be, or you know your systems are messy or non-existent.

However, letting people help you with your business may be one of the smartest strategies you'll have.

There are so many businesses that provide help to other businesses. They may offer bookkeeping services, social media support, policy and procedure development, marketing and so on.

They know very well that what a business looks like at the front can be very very different from the back. And for them, that can be a good thing because it allows them to make a valued difference to your business.

They can see what is working, what isn't, and help implement changes to make your business life easier and more successful. That's what they do. And there is so much demand for their work because business owners can't be great at all the back end tasks within their business.

When businesses provide business support services as a contractor, virtually (not on your premises), we call them Virtual Assistants. In truth, they are simply part of the Virtual Assistant Industry which includes business to business providers such as web developers, copywriters, online business managers, business consultants and much more.

And what's important to note is that all of these businesses within the Virtual Assistant Industry also need help with their businesses. They need to focus on supporting you and working in their zone of genius. And to ensure they can do that they also need to outsource to other providers.

We all know that it's better to be a Master of One than a Jack of all Trades. When we try to do everything we end up doing them all at a mediocre level instead of doing one thing really well. In business, you need to be a Master of One. Know what you are incredible at. Know what lights you up. And outsource the rest.

My Virtual Insights

As someone who proudly calls herself 'unemployable', I have found my constantly evolving business to be my pride and joy now for 15 years. Never did I think that this would be what my future held. But when I was in high school we didn't even have the Internet so the concept of running an online community supporting virtual assistants wasn't even imaginable.

Growing up I didn't really think about being self-employed either. My ideas were around marine biology, disability support, support work in third world countries or perhaps something animal related like veterinarian. I soon found out I have not got the stomach for vet work and I hated science, so that ruled out marine biology or a vet career.

I did end up doing some work for a few months in Kenya but I really felt that without a big organization behind me I couldn't achieve much or make any kind of impact that I'd dreamed of. And my homesickness levels were legendary.

So after a few years working in various admin and reception jobs I started working in the disability sector. And I loved it. It was great. I also volunteered with Kids Under Kanvas (a day trip and camping program for kids with disabilities), with the RSPCA, with St Johns Ambulance, Rotary and doing wildlife rescue. In my job I worked up to middle management and then when the opportunity to work for myself as a VA came along I gave it a go. I never knew where it would take me.

And what a journey it's been! I have met incredible people. I have worked with the most creative and interesting people. I have also worked with total twits and met some massively anti-social business owners. I've seen business owners copy each other, belittle each other and lie to each other. But I've also seen incredible support, companionship, collaborations and friendships. It's been full of highs and lows. And the learning never ends.

But what I've learnt so far about working with VAs is what I want to share with you here in this book. When I started my business I thought all business owners were intimidating, rich, and smart. I put them on a pedestal. When I was employed I saw upper management the same way – there was always the hierarchy that guided all processes.

After years of working with business owners, I now feel way more comfortable in a room full of business owners than I do in a room full of employees! I know that business owners are simply human beings trying to create something awesome, doing the hard work, learning all they can, trying things out and winning, and trying other things out and losing. And at the end of the day we all simply need to communicate well and be kind to each other. And hopefully this book will help you do a bit more of that while building up a team to help you with that awesome creation of yours.

The Virtual Insights

One of the things I wanted to provide you with in this book was insights and tips from amazing business owners who have outsourced in their businesses – their outsourcing secrets.

To achieve this I contacted some business owners who I've seen really step into their own in business and who were happy to share their thoughts on outsourcing. I sent them a few questions to guide their contributions to this book and that is how the 'Virtual Insights' peppered throughout this book were made.

I hope you enjoy reading their stories as much as I have. Every business is unique and every business owner has their own way of doing things. Rather than just reading about the how-to from my perspective, learning what others have done, what worked and what didn't, will hopefully give you a more colourful virtual insight into outsourcing for your business. In fact, I think we have one coming up now...

Virtual Insights by Hannah Naylor

Effortless Eco

effortlesseco.com.au

Hey there! I'm Hannah and I am the head honcho at Effortless Eco. I spend my time working to design and manufacture eco-friendly products.

When I decided I needed some help from a VA I knew I wanted to stick with someone in Australia. I wanted someone who could understand my personality, my time restrictions, and would be available to talk to when needed - without worrying too much about time zones. At the moment I have two different VAs. One does a lot of writing for my website, and edits my blogs - she understands my voice and my quirks. The second VA is also a writer, but she focuses on policy writing – the sort of writing that makes me want to avoid doing it for the rest of eternity.

I've learned that VAs are simply amazing. If there is ever anything I don't want to do - BOOM my VA does it for me. All of those life sapping tasks I hate, I don't do them anymore, because lets face it, life is short, its takes less time and therefore less money for a professional to do it.

My biggest tip would be — get your pitch right. Make sure you are specific in your needs/prefered contact method/personality type. Then a VA will find you, and it might even be love at first email.

WHAT IS A VIRTUAL ASSISTANT?

A VIRTUAL ASSISTANT or Virtual Contractor is a business owner who specialises in a business support service and offers that service remotely (at least most of the time).

This is a pretty broad description and if you start to think about it, you'll quickly realise that this would include businesses such as bookkeepers, social media strategists, marketers, copywriters, graphic designers, Online Business Managers (OBMs), web developers, speakers' assistants, author assistants, transcriptionists, workflow and automation experts, remote receptionists and so much more – see list at the end of this book.

For this book, we will always be referring to self-employed contractors when we refer to VAs or VCs.

Many people confuse Virtual Staff with Virtual Assistants, and yes, they often use the same title. So to clarify, a VA or VC is self-employed, manages their accounts and taxes, manages their superannuation, sick leave or any other entitlements, and also works for other clients. You are not their employer – you are their client.

A Virtual Staff member is just that. Often based in the Philippines or India, they work through a larger recruitment agency who oversees your business relationship and is responsible for the resulting outcomes. For example, Renee has a Virtual Staff member, Sol, who she introduced us to in the Foreword.

There are possibly hundreds of thousands of Virtual Assistants throughout the world. They are very popular in the US, UK, Australia, New Zealand, South African and parts of Europe. Some VAs in the Philippines and India are self-employed too and do not work through an agency. This book explores mostly Australian Virtual Assistants as that's the area I've worked most closely with, however you'll find that there are many similarities from country to country.

Virtual Insights by Jenny De Lacy

The Visibility Coach

thevisibilitycoach.com.au

I hired my first VA (offshore) in late 2017 with a sense of great excitement! Here is the savior of all my time wasting on social media woes, the heroine to make me a more productive business person! Hoorah! But just like any additional employee, a VA needs nurture and to connect, open lines of communication, clear instructions and processes. And I know now, that if I don't have them in place, the value of outsourcing diminishes rapidly!

So I changed focus, and found a more senior support person nearby, to set up my processes with me, sort me out and help me focus. When I'm ready I'll get another team member.

What I have learnt is that you need clear processes, and time to build a relationship, but when you know WHAT you need, it will help choose the right person. There's no such thing as going out and 'just get a VA' – there's more to it than that.

WHAT CAN VAS DO?

WHEN THE VA INDUSTRY started, they were business owners, mainly women, offering administrative support from home.

Emails and the Internet had just started, but large files were impossible to send that way. So, a lot of the work was saved to disks and delivered to and from the client by car or post, depending on the distance.

My first experience with a Virtual Assistant was when I was an Office Manager, and I had to take some tapes to a nearby home to be transcribed. When they were ready, I went and picked them up again. These days the whole process would be transferred via something like Dropbox.

The modern Virtual Assistant is better described by the term Virtual Contractor because it covers all contractors who provided business to business service, virtually.

When you think about business-related contractors, you'd commonly think of copywriters, web designers and developers, bookkeepers, graphic designers, social media managers and strategists, and even virtual receptionists. The list is extremely long. VAs also do tender applications, event management, webinars, transcription, video editing, proofreading, CRM management, workflows, automation, cold calling, diary management – you name it; they'd do it. If it's for your business and can be done off-site, it falls under the VA banner.

As business owners, we generally start our businesses so we can work on something we are passionate about and so we can call the shots and have more flexibility. But when we try to do everything ourselves, we find ourselves doing the exact opposite. We become shackled to our business and have no flexibility, no fun and feeling like we are not in control at all.

That's because running a business is so much more than providing a product or a solution. There's so much that needs to be done around the product/solution to attract and deliver to our clients.

I like to think we are moving past the days where people feel they have to 'hustle'. The days where people feel guilty if they don't answer "Busy!" to the question "How's life?".

I also look forward to the days when more people embrace a life where they love what they work on, and they don't solely work to make mega money, where a successful business is classified by one that provides enough opportunity to the owner and their family to enjoy the simple things in life.

Having a team to help you in business can assist you with whatever goals you have. Whether it's to have more time and flexibility or to make more money – having other people working on the things you aren't loving or amazing at, allows you to create a business that ticks whatever goals you've set for it.

Virtual Insights by Kate Toon

The Recipe for SEO Success
The Clever Copywriting School

katetoon.com

My name is Kate Toon, and I've been running my business for about 11 years (if feels longer some days).

I have two core businesses:

- **The Recipe for SEO Success**, where I teach small business folk, marketers, copywriters, designers, bloggers and store owners how to grapple the Google beast and drive more traffic and conversions through their websites
- **The Clever Copywriting School**, where I teach would-be and established copywriters how to be better copywriters.

I also have three podcasts and large Facebook groups, run a conference, speak around the world, and have subscription-based membership products.

I feel tired just writing this.

I started using a virtual assistant (VA) about five years ago when I expanded from just offering services one-to-one to creating passive income products. I started with a local Australian VA who was amazing. When she moved on

WHAT CAN VAS DO?

at short notice it left me a little burned, and I managed without one.

But around two years ago the wonderful Rosie connected me with Leanne Woff, an Australian VA. And she's been the best thing to happen to my business. We've used overseas VAs here and there, but I prefer to work with Leanne and her team.

I now get over 30 hours a week of support.

Obviously Australian VAs are much more expensive, which makes it a luxury for some. But the advantages are huge.

Even though overseas VAs can have a great grasp of English and be highly trained, there's a lack of connection when it comes to slang, idioms and humour. Something's just missing. (Or at least that's how it was for me.) I know many people have nothing but praise for their overseas VAs.

My Big Learnings

I've had several big learnings along the way about working with a VA:

- **Trust:** It took me a long time to just let my VA get on with things and not micromanage every task. Like many, I struggle to let go. My business is very tied to my identity, and so letting someone do things for me was difficult. It came to the crunch when I started travelling more for speaking gigs. I just had to let go and let Leanne do the work.

And she did such a good job I never took the work back.

- **Communication**: The best thing for Leanne and I is when we chat face-to-face over Zoom (or ideally in person). We try to meet up as often as we can. Emails and Slack messages just don't cut it sometimes.
- **Support**: I feel Leanne is genuinely involved and passionate about my business. She really cares. And I care about her success too. I give her heaps of shoutouts, and refer clients to her. I want her to be successful, even if it means she may one day move on. (Sob.)

My Top Tips

1. Make sure you document everything you need done. I found making Loom videos a great way to pass on training.

2. Ensure your VA is available when you need them. If they're working out of hours this may cause frustration.

3. Use a project management tool to organise projects. We use Asana and Slack to avoid sending emails back and forth.

4. Ensure you work hard on the relationship. Be patient and kind, reward good work, and promote and support your VA. Good communication is everything.

5. Understand that it will take up to three months for them to fully learn your processes from end to end (depending on the complexity).

6. Realise it takes time to trust. At first, asking for itemised lists of what's been done is fine. Over time you may feel less inclined to micromanage and be able to let go completely.

Stay tooned!

WHY WOULD YOU OUTSOURCE?

PEOPLE WHO OUTSOURCE generally end up with four key benefits. They are Direction, Support, Growth & Freedom. Let's explore those.

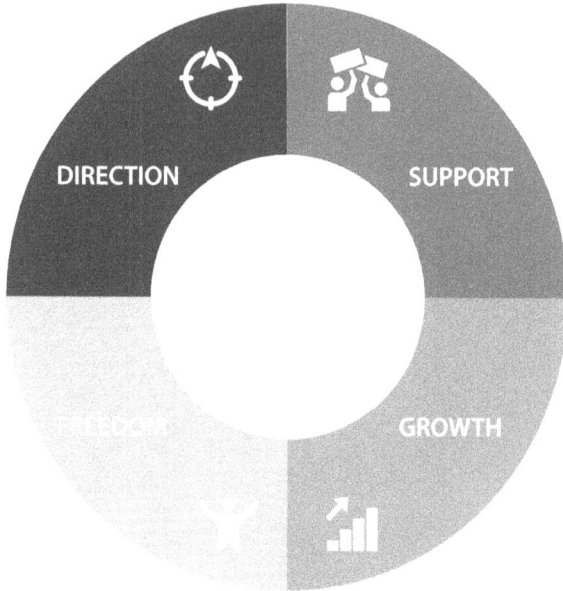

Direction

When you're lacking direction, you also end up lacking drive, passion and focus. And this isn't a good place to be in!

In business, you need to be self-driven to keep going, have passion to get through the rough patches, and focus to ensure you are moving forward in the right direction. Without these it can all get too hard very quickly.

When you have direction you feel empowered, confident, determined and inspired by your business and this makes the journey more satisfying and rewarding.

Direction allows you to make smarter decisions, more quickly. You can see more easily what fits into the map you've drawn and what doesn't, and quickly assess your next steps.

Support

With support, you have access to more skills, more time, more feedback. You have people there who can lift you when you need it and who can fill the skill gaps you have. With support, you can do more, faster. You can even do more, faster and better!

A really common situation for small business owners is when they find themselves burnt out. They are working on everything and it's taking all of their time.

At this stage it's worth stopping and taking some time to work out which tasks bring you joy or bring you money versus the tasks that I call 'LSTs' – these are the 'Life Sapping Tasks'. They are necessary but they don't directly bring the money in, don't bring you joy and don't really need to be done by YOU.

To work this out grab a piece of paper or jump onto a spreadsheet and put all of your tasks into the first column.

Make 2 columns to the right and put one of them how many hours per week or month you spend on that activity and then in the next column how much money this activity is worth to you per hour. After that you can have a tally column which calculates the number of hours by the hourly value.

Next, make 4 more columns to the right and title them each a positive emotion that resonates with you. For example, happy, creative, accomplished, challenged. Think about what emotions you WANT to be feeling in your business.

Then give each task a score out of 5 for each emotion. Does the task make you feel happy, creative, accomplished and challenged. Add up the score and pop that into the last column.

You can sort the list according to the value in the last column to see which tasks bring you the most joy. Compare the level of joy to the number of hours you spend working on that task. How many hours a week or month, or even year do you spend on tasks that bring you no joy? Do they bring in money? What are you noticing about how you spend your time?

Here's an example of how that would look:

Tasks	Hours per week	Value per hour	Total value	Happy	Creative	Accomplished	Challenged	Total
Answering phones	4	$0	$0	0	0	2	2	4
Creating new content	10	$0	$0	5	5	5	5	20
Mentoring	5	$90	$450	5	4	5	4	18

Being smart about your time and understanding the value or where you spend it is important. Working on things you love balanced with things that bring in the money is what works for me. If I don't get joy from it but I know it's important – I'll outsource it.

Looking at the table above you can see that the business owner loves content creation. They may need to make the initial content with the added value that they enjoy it, but they may find it beneficial to outsource the repurposing of that same content to better leverage their content and effort.

Likewise they love mentoring, but what about setting up those mentoring sessions and following up?

This is where the support of a team is so valuable. Having a brains trust to tap into when you need it will help your business grow faster and have more impact.

Growth

With direction and support, you'll achieve more growth. You'll be able to focus on the activities that bring the biggest results and support your customers in a more effective, strategic way. You'll find that with a team around you, you are more accountable and tend to be more active when it comes to working towards your goals.

This is where you start to really scale and work smarter in business.

Freedom

And finally, imagine having direction, support and growth. You'll be able to find more freedom to do what you created your business for in the first place. Whether it's the freedom to create the impact you desire, the freedom to raise your family comfortably, or the freedom to pick and chose how you work and who you work with. Heaven!

Virtual Insights by Emily Chadbourne

Your Mindset Coach | Unashamedly Human

emilychadbourne.com

My name is Emily Chadbourne and I used to be a bit of an idiot. Okay, a total idiot. It's a whole story but for the purpose of this book, The Outsourcing Secret, all you need to know for now is that 3 years ago I was waiting tables for a living earning $20 an hour and hating life.

One day I realised I couldn't do life alone. I had huge gaps in my knowledge and abilities in basic humaning (not a word but I'm using it anyway) so I began to learn about how to change my thinking and so change my feelings and actions to manifest in a different reality for myself.

Now I have the honour of teaching other humans the same formula for success.

Interestingly but also predictably, the same realisations I had as a waitress have applied in my entrepreneurial journey.

I can't do business alone. And I have huge gaps in my knowledge and abilities.

Especially when it comes to administration, structure and basically anything to do with the back of house systems I need to generate consistent cash flow and happy clients.

I tried to do everything myself for the first 2 years in business. I thought I was being time efficient (who has the time to get organised?) and economical (I'll just do it myself).

It was scrappy and messy at best and it was really limiting my growth.

I had a great mentor in my early days of business who once said to me "Em, don't bother spending effort trying to improve at the things you don't enjoy or aren't good at. Instead, find the thing that you love and excel at, and become masterful at it." I wish I'd listened to him sooner.

Outsourcing to my Australian based VA has been the best financial decision I could have made for my business.

I no longer have a desktop that looks like Word threw up on it.

I can find my files easily and when I do they look professional because my VA has formatted them. My resources used to look like my 4 year old niece had an argument with Canva.

I don't miss things anymore and I have systems in place which look after me and my clients.

But it's more than the professional look and the time saved.

New projects which had been thoughts for so long have now come to life because my VA brings new perspective, contacts (she has a great network) and a certain level of accountability. I need to manage my VA which in turn means I need to execute a stricter discipline over my own time management and delivery.

It is true that life is not a solo sport. Running out onto the pitch alone is a foolish move and a tough game to play. In my experience outsourcing the bits I don't do well to someone who does has given me the time, money and energy to do what I do best in my business.

Here are my top 3 tips for outsourcing (and funnily enough, they can also be applied to every other area of life!)

Be clear

I once read a Brene Brown quote that said "to be clear is to be kind" and it is so true. I have seen people get outsourcing really wrong because they have assumed that their VA is inside their head. They're not. That would be weird and gross. We are all human and just because you know what you mean, or you can see what you want it to look like doesn't mean everyone else does. Be clear. Double check. And then check again.

Be kind

It's weird that this is even a point but it's so valid. We are naturally egocentric as creatures, it's survival at its most basic but it also creeps into our leadership. When we own our own business, we naturally feel protective and want to keep in control of the baby we've so far managed to drag up. But asking someone to come on board and help get our business to the next level requires us to take feedback (I get it, no one wants to hear their baby is ugly).

When we feel shame (this bit of my baby is ugly) it is our instinct to blame to protect our ego. All of a sudden, it's our VA's fault that a link isn't working, or they didn't understand the brief. We go into panic mode and forget to be kind. Be clear. Be kind.

Be honest

This one was a tough one for me. My overriding desire to people please and avoid confrontation meant I would often say YES when I meant NO.

It went like this.

- External voice: "That colour is fine."
  Internal voice: "How did they make a colour so bad?"
- External voice: "Wednesday is fine."
  Internal voice: "I need it by Monday."
- External voice: "I thought I sent you that email."
  Internal voice: "I definitely didn't send that email."

Leadership and collaboration requires us to be a grown up. Always do what is best (not easiest) for the business but also make sure that both you and your team (your VA) are supported, secure and happy. It's a skill. And I don't claim to get it right all the time but that's why I think it's important to find a VA you respect, who fills in the blanks you leave and makes you laugh. Because business, just like life, is meant to be fun.

GETTING TO THIS POINT IN YOUR BUSINESS

IF YOU HAVE A DREAM for your business, one that includes growth, flexibility, exposure, or whatever definition of success you chose, imagine achieving it on your own. Is it possible? Is it smart? Or would working with a team be a better vessel to get you there.

When you're doing everything yourself, you may find

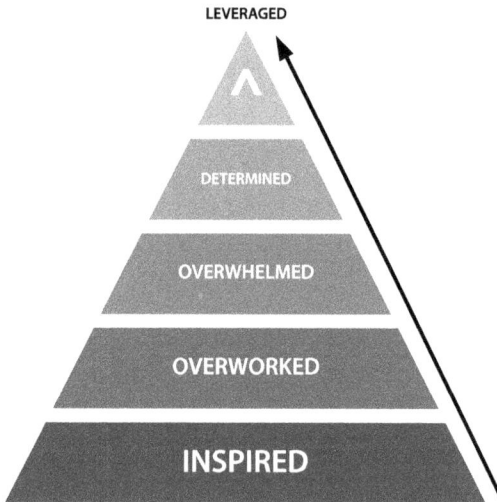

LEVERAGED

∧

DETERMINED

OVERWHELMED

OVERWORKED

INSPIRED

yourself multitasking ALL THE TIME. This is terrible for productivity – our brain isn't built to work efficiently on multiple things.

Guy Winch, PhD, author of Emotional First Aid: Practical Strategies for Treating Failure, Rejection, Guilt and Other Everyday Psychological Injuries says that 'task-switching', which is what multitasking really is, wastes productivity because your attention is expended on the act of switching gears—plus, you never get fully 'in the zone' for either activity.

In the mid-1990s, Robert Rogers, PhD, and Stephen Monsell, D.Phil, found that even when people had to switch completely predictably between two tasks every two or four trials, they were still slower on task-switch than on task-repeat trials.

Add to that the fact that we are naturally slower at completing tasks that we're not great at, doing everything yourself is an expensive habit – costing time, energy and money.

Therefore it would be fair to assume that when you allow yourself the time and space you need to work on the things you love, your productivity, energy and results all naturally improve.

Having seen so many people start and grow their businesses, I've noticed them working through the following stages.

Inspired

When you start your business, it's so exciting. Scary sometimes, but exciting. You've got this great idea and the vision to make it work for you and to achieve your version of success and freedom. You get advice from everyone, you look back at employed life and laugh at the insanity of it all – now you can do what you want when you want!

You have visions of working the hours you want and only working with clients who you love. You imagine spending your hours working on the tasks that excite you the most. You'll have this great income, and you'll be feeling pretty damn proud of the great business masterpiece you've created.

You work out a business name, a list of all the services you could offer, maybe a website or social media page and you tell everyone you are the one they need.

Overworked

However, once you've started and have been working for a little while you may find yourself becoming overworked. You're running your business, but it's getting hectic.

You're making ok money but know that if you had a little more time you could be achieving a lot more. You know you're being held back by tasks that other people could do – and they could probably do it faster and better. The LSTs are hijacking your day!

You're not getting the time you need to work in your zone of genius. You feel like you rarely get to do what you love most.

But you don't have TIME to tell people how to do it for you. And you don't have the money either. It's all just easier to keep plodding along and doing it yourself. One day you'll have the time. One day you'll have the money.

How many things have you done in your life that took a little time to set up but paid off in the long run? Building a home, saving to buy a car, building a veggie garden – all things that take time but afterwards, they give you the freedom to reap the benefits.

Our lives are full of these scenarios but when it comes to outsourcing, many resist. It's interesting to note that most people outsource the care of their child more easily than they outsource the care of their business.

Overwhelmed

You decide that you're going to invest the time and money into getting some support. We all love leverage. We love achieving more by doing less. We love achieving more by working on the stuff we love. And outsourcing is one of the best ways to achieve this.

But it's scary.

There are so many apparent solutions out there and so many VAs. How do you pick the right one? What do you get them to work on? What do you need to have set up in your business first?

It may feel like the chicken and egg dilemma – you feel you need to tidy your business up before you get a VA in to help you tidy your business up.

You ask online for support and hear from hundreds of VAs and discover that sorting through those responses would be just another huge task you simply can't get to. It all feels very overwhelming.

Determined

But with the right guidance, you realise it doesn't have to be that hard. Once you start, I assure you, you'll start loving it. Your creation, your business, gets stronger and more beautiful when you can put into it what you want. When you can spend your days in your zone of genius you can start building more revenue. You feel happier because you're not spending time on things that drain you. You have more time for the other things in life. You can start to remove the shackles of a one-person-business.

At this stage, you need to get clear on your goals, your strengths and your weaknesses and what you need to fill any gaps. You need to have clarity around who could support you in what capacity in your business. With the right information (this book for example!), you start to get the ball rolling in the right direction.

Leveraged

While outsourcing means other people get to see your 'business undies' – the behind the scenes stuff which isn't always as glamorous as you'd like them to believe – it also means you have more knowledge, experience, opportunities and perspectives available to you. And this is seriously valuable stuff.

Now that you've let the right people into the 'inner sanctum' you've realised that they can do so many things you don't need to do anymore. You've freed up space in your mind and your calendar to focus on what's important, what pushes things forward. You have room to think and be creative.

Not only that, but you can tap into their collective minds which provides you with so many more options and ideas. You have people who understand what you are trying to achieve and they are totally on board!

You can make more money, be more effective and efficient – you're able to get seriously leveraged!

In my business I'm proud to be working the hours I want – over the past year it's been 2 days a week with a few extra hours here and there if I felt like it – making the money I want. My business is now turning over 6 figures even though I'm working less hours than previously –

simply because I'm working smarter and leveraging through outsourcing.

Virtual Insights by Caroline Kropack

Brownie Designer | Brazen Brownies

brazenbrownies.com.au

I'm the owner of a small but growing food business. The food business is a tough game, and my weary feet at the end of long days in the kitchen can certainly attest to that. But I'm fortunate in the sense that I truly do love what I do.

I started off 3 years ago as a home-based business, leaving a 20+ year legal career behind and baking brownies out of my home kitchen, which I wholesaled to local stores. I now operate 2 retail shops where I manufacture and sell my brownies, together with a range of gelato also made on premises. I'm still very hands-on in my kitchens, where I spend long hours, so my ability to perform administrative tasks has become increasingly limited.

At various stages I've had the need for specialised help in a range of areas. I've always managed to do my own bookkeeping, but with an ever-increasing list of other critical tasks required to grow my business.

I could no longer justify trying to do 'everything' myself.

That was when I first reached out to Rosie Shilo and her team of VAs.

From what started as a referral for the simple job of compiling email addresses for a database, I sought subsequent referrals from Rosie for other VAs skilled in all kinds of areas.

Copywriting, form design and building, website development, social media, applications, direct marketing strategies. To be able to outsource certain aspects of my business that were challenging me and tying up my valuable time, came as such a huge relief. The cost-benefit was enormous, not to mention a preservation of my sanity.

For any business owner contemplating outsourcing a task or project, I would encourage you to sit down with pen and paper (yes, we may live in a 'virtual' world but there are still some things that are sacred!). Try to count up the hours you realistically believe are required for YOU to complete that particular task or project. Factor in your own degree of knowledge of the subject matter or task, and your skill set and level of competence. Then add a weighting factor for sanity preservation and life-work balance if you didn't actually have to do that task yourself. Get an accurate as possible estimate of the costs associated with engaging a VA, and if the numbers stack up, outsource!

WHAT DO YOU NEED?

TO CREATE a leveraged business that's allowing you to have (or keep walking towards) an impact and the freedom you seek, you need a few key ingredients. These are areas that businesses who have leverage have mastered and keep strengthening.

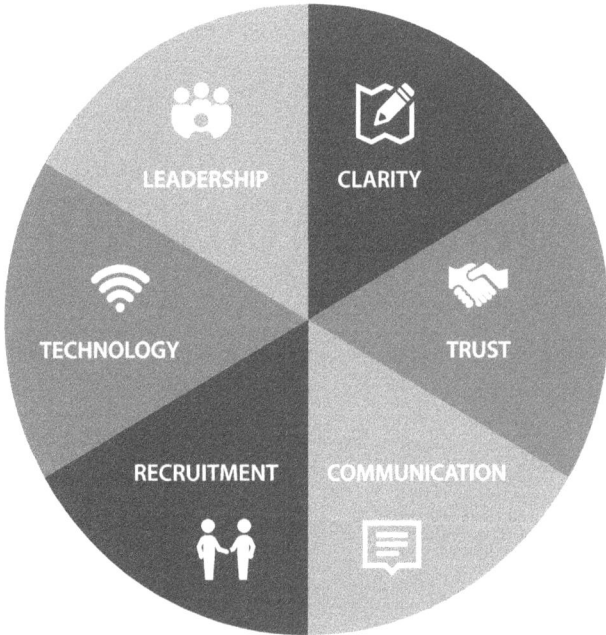

You don't have to go to too much effort in preparing your own business before outsourcing if you know what you want and can communicate that well.

Not everything needs to be tidy – a VA can help clean up as they work through projects. Having access to the Internet to be able to share files and send emails is a must – but otherwise, the most important thing is to know what you want and need. Often when you know what you want, you can also work out exactly what you need when you chat with your contractor.

You also need to speak to your business accountant and lawyer to make sure your business structure and policies are sound. You need to be responsible for the security of your business just as much as the contractor.

Below are the keys to successful outsourcing.

Clarity

You need to have a solid product that has demand. Pretty simple to start with, but important. If you don't know your product or demand, it's best you start with a business coach to get some clarity around what you're offering. The beauty of this is that you don't need this BEFORE you start working with a VA. You can enlist the help of a VA to get clarity around this through consulting, research and development depending on the specialty of the VA.

Speaking of clarity, you need to be clear about where you want to go with your business. Why are you doing it? Do you have a big enough 'why' to keep you focused and passionate? Do you have big goals and mini goals to work towards? How are you planning on reaching those goals? What skills do you have to reach them and which skills are currently lacking?

Trust - Letting Go

This is the bit I love. You have skills and a vision. But the odds of you having the all of the skills and time you need to bring the vision to fruition are pretty slim. There are so many aspects to running a successful business; no-one can do all of them well and quickly while maintaining any level of sanity.

Add to this that more people (the RIGHT people) can bring new perspectives, ideas, contacts and resources to the table – very valuable stuff.

People can form part of your inner team or contribute in other ways. For example, they may be someone you admire, someone you can bounce ideas off or someone you can learn from. Building your community is a smart strategy for business growth.

As Michael Griffiths, the Referral Marketing Guru says:

"It's very simple – you cannot grow your business unless you leverage other people. Simply put, you need to build a team in order for you to really be able to grow and scale.

For most business owners they are the bottleneck in their business and the sooner they hand off tasks to other people the sooner they can concentrate on doing the 'A' activities.

Virtual assistants are a simple first step, with very low risk of overheads, to take your first step of growth. Your business is only as successful as the things you hand off to others, so you can focus on evolving your model, systems and sales."

Anyone who has had to employ staff or work in a team knows that it can be hard to manage others effectively. Managing a team remotely has extra hurdles and more demand for communication skills.

When the project you're managing is your business, your very own dream, it becomes personal, and that can make letting go very very hard. I call this 'showing your biz undies' – letting other people into the inner sanctum of your business, which most likely isn't as glamourous as you'd like them to think it is.

But with the right vision, strategy and techniques, you should be able to let go and build something wonderful.

Most people imagine that everyone else has beautiful documentation and systems in place for their business. Business owners have things under control, don't they? Those who don't have all of their t's crossed and I's dotted wonder if they're frauds or if they'll look silly and unprofessional to an outsider if they let them in.

There are two things I think are important to realise.

1. Pretty much everyone has a bit of a schmozzle going on with their business processes and administration. If they're doing everything themselves, it makes sense that not everything will be perfect because they're not going to be experts at the many facets of running a business. And the longer you work by yourself, the more this can get out of hand. But it's never too late to ask for help.

2. When you know what your zone of genius is, it's easier to release the other things. Understanding what your strengths and weaknesses are is seriously valuable stuff. Don't sweat the stuff you don't rock at – give it to someone else who sits in THEIR zone of genius doing it.

Communication

In a world where we communicate online almost as much as we take breaths, you'd think we'd all be great at it. But we're not. We know the functional side of communicating online – most people can use emails, social media, phone and messaging services – but communicating effectively is a whole different skill set. And without good communication skills, outsourcing can become very challenging.

As with any management role, being able to communicate clearly and respectfully is of paramount importance. Without careful consideration, a quick text message can be interpreted incorrectly, and either feelings are hurt, or tasks are mismanaged.

Unlike conventional Face 2 Face management roles, virtual roles often require clear written and verbal communication. That's when we notice how important facial expressions and body language are in this process. Without them, pieces of the message can be misconstrued. If you don't have good virtual communication skills, you would need to work on that before you outsource.

Business owners are passionate and skilled in a set area. Knowing what programs are available for managing business communication and processes is very often not a skill or interest they have. Many VAs love this sort of thing. So, if there are fears around what systems to use to communicate effectively, speak to the virtual provider you want to work with, and see what they can recommend. Many online CRMs (Client Relationship Management Software) have built-in task lists, emails, calendars etc. so that you can keep track of who is doing what, for whom, and when.

Ensuring a communication match

It's important to be clear with your VA about what your style of communication is and your preferred methods. This is one of the reasons why I recommend having a phone chat, a Skype chat and email correspondence all before making your decision.

By communication style, I mean what, of the following styles, best describes you:

- Straight talker
- Vague and in need of direction
- Easily distracted by lots of ideas on the go at once
- Avoids confrontation
- Uses humour
- Quiet
- Loud
- And so on

Preferred methods could include:

- Phone
- Email
- Face to Face
- Skype
- Messenger/SMS
- And so on

Being honest about this upfront will help you find the right VA for you. Sometimes opposite communication styles fit together well. However, you do need to be on the same page about methods. If you hate the phone and your VA prefers it – it's going to cause issues.

The next thing is to be very clear with your contractor about what you want to achieve and how you plan on getting there. Skype chats can be great for having these conversations. You can even use the spreadsheets you'll create later in this book.

There are software programs (see 'technology') which can help manage task lists, projects, clients etc. and are very useful for ensuring you both know what each other is doing without micromanaging and checking in too often. Some of the programs I've heard a lot about include Asana, Trello, Basecamp and Teamwork. All are useful for collaborating.

Avoid the trap of using too many systems. Keep it simple! Over the years I feel like I've tried every CRM under the sun. I've finally stuck with the same CRM now for almost 2 years. I currently use Ontraport which manages all of my client information, newsletters, payments and forms. I manage tasks and projects in Google Sheets, most of which my team have access to.

I asked my dear friend and fellow business owner Monique Eddy from A Virtual Copywriting Monstar to write up her tips for communicating effectively with your VA and I've included it below. It's important to note that not all VAs will be working with you long term. Some are one-off projects or come on board for more adhoc support as needed. For those who are there to support you in an ongoing manner with tasks such as your LSTs and business management, the following steps are a great guide.

How to communicate clearly with your VA

Guest Contributor – Monique Eddy

Finding your ideal VA is a bit like dating. You've looked at a few online sites, checked out profiles and visited websites. You've done some stalking, sussed out their social media, and you've read what others have said. Heck, you may have even sent a few messages to see what type of response you receive.

And then you decide to swipe right and keep your fingers crossed that they're everything they've said they are.

We've all heard the stories of people getting scammed online. It happens, and it sucks.

So, how do you know that your VA can do what they say?

You start a conversation

It's as easy as that. I'm a BIG believer that when you're choosing a VA, you need to set some time aside to talk to them. Not email, not Messenger, and not snaps!

Set a time with your prospective VA for a phone call. Or even better, try a Skype call so you can see your new VA in person.

The name itself shows that VAs are virtual, but this doesn't mean they need to be a faceless, voiceless person at the other end of an email. And it's when you talk to someone, that you can get a feel for their personality.

I mean, you wouldn't commit to a relationship without speaking to the person, would you? You're about to show your business undies (a term commonly used by Rosie to reflect your business back-end) to your VA, so you want to make sure you're at least compatible.

So please, make your first point of contact with a potential VA a phone call.

Here's a quick checklist of what to listen out for:

- Do they listen to you and answer your questions precisely?
- Are they letting you finish your sentence or are they talking over you?
- Do they respond to your manner – i.e. if you laugh or say something funny, do they also laugh?
- Can they confidentially describe what they do and offer solutions to help your business?
- Are you feeling any connection – does the conversation flow easily?

After you've spoken to a VA, if you've got any doubts, remember there are huge networks of VAs in Australia all wanting to find their ideal client. So perhaps as a business owner, you need to not only search for a VA but think about who your ideal VA would be.

Once you've found your perfect VA, there are so many ways you can communicate with them. Let's explore this.

Virtual Communication with your VA

Virtual communication isn't hard. We all do it. And if we're honest, we probably communicate more online than in person these days.

It's so easy to send someone a quick text message, a quick Facebook message, a quick Snap. We're all super busy, and we don't seem to have time for a long sit-down phone call with anyone.

And that's fine – for our mates.

But when it comes to working with a VA, a quick online message may not always cut it.

The key to building a successful client/VA relationship is clear communication.

What you need to remember is that your VA isn't sitting in your office, waiting for your instructions, and watching you explain what needs doing as you're running through the task.

When you're starting with your VA, be prepared for a stage of 'onboarding'. During this time, you'll need to be giving clear instructions.

Don't stress – this stage will pass once your new VA has seen how you run your business, put processes in place (or follow yours if you have any), and become an integral part of your business. Give it a month or two.

One thing I've learnt in my many years in running a virtual business is that we're not mind readers, and most of us don't have magical crystal balls. Shock horror hey! It would be seriously awesome if we were psychically in-tune with our clients. You'd truly find another you to run your business if this was the case!

But give it time. Once you've worked with the same VA for years, you'll find that they're running your business and doing things before you've even thought about it!

So, let's have a look at the best ways to communicate throughout your VA journey.

The Dating Stage

At the start of any relationship, you're talking all the time. You're getting to know each other, and you find there's so much to talk about.

Your VA will need to have access to you. Your VA is a fellow business owner and will pick things up quickly. However, the early stages require a little bit of patience and making yourself available to answer questions. Remember, it will make sense to you as it's your business, but your VA is new to your business.

Think of yourself as a teacher. You set your students a task to complete, and you're sure to get some questions if something isn't quite clear enough. Some will pick it up and run with it, troubleshooting as they go, but others will prefer to ask questions.

In these early days, phone calls, Skype calls (with video or screen sharing) or detailed emails are your vital communication methods. I highly suggest you ask your VA their preferred communication method. Is it the same as yours? If you love talking, but your VA loves emailing, you may not be a perfect match.

Whatever method you choose, tasks need to be clearly set, with instructions given.

Quick tip: If you've already got a procedure manual, give this to your VA for some 'light' reading. This will help them understand the tasks. If you don't have a procedure manual, ask your VA to document all the instructions you're giving. Keep adding to this and voila – you've got a procedure manual that explains how to run your business.

There are also some fantastic task management programs available. Most VAs in the forums use and recommend Asana, Insightly, Trello, Zoho and Teamwork, but there are loads available.

If you're using a task management program that your VA doesn't use, give them a quick training session. Or if you don't have one and your VA uses one, let them give you a quick training session!

These programs are the best for keeping track of tasks, communicating where you're both at, and keeping projects flowing.

Setting up processes like this from the start could save you loads of time in the future. This will still require extra communication during the early stages to provide additional instruction to your new VA.

The Engagement Stage

You now know enough about your VA, you know you work well together, and you've accepted them as part of your business.

You've also worked through all the initial teething problems, worked out how you both communicate well with each other and have processes in place.

After you've been working with your VA for a little while, you should find that they can now handle simple instructions, know what needs doing on a day to day basis, and basically can run your business without much input for you.

In a nutshell, you're a great match and others may have even told you how much better your business is running now.

It's during this stage that you'll find communication gets a bit easier. Your VA won't need as much contact with you. Of course, if you start up new projects, this may change, but for your day to day tasks, your VA should know what to do.

There will always be occasions where your VA will need to run something by you, but they won't need to take up much of your time to get their answer.

Your communication would include using a task management program (if that's what you put into place from the beginning), quick emails or phone calls, and you may even start using Facebook messages if you're that way inclined.

Quick tip on email subject headers: Although your VA will have a dedicated email and inbox purely for your business, it may be full of enquiries and emails from your clients. If you have an urgent job you need help with or have important instructions for your VA; please be clear. For example, 'URGENT JOB: Needed by COB on Wednesday', or 'INSTRUCTIONS: A change to our phone answering procedure'.

It's during your engagement stage that you should start feeling comfortable with your VA, trusting them and being able to talk freely with them. You may even find yourself sharing life stories with them.

The Marriage Stage

When you've reached this stage, you and your VA have made it! You'll work together for years to come. You've worked out all your processes, and now everything flows beautifully.

It's also at this stage where you may not communicate quite as much as you used to. Don't get me wrong, you'll still talk, but it'll be little catch ups around your work. You will know each other so well that you'll have an unspoken understanding of what you both need to do to keep your relationship ticking along.

By this stage, your VA should understand your gibberish (and you'll understand theirs). Your instructions, although at times brief, will be crystal clear to your VA, and their brief responses won't sound like a brush off, but as a sign they know what they're doing.

It's at this stage where you have found that magical crystal ball!

Your VA will be performing all the routine tasks without input from you, and may even be thinking beyond the day to day and telling you about things that will benefit your business. They'd be looking for opportunities for your business and be an integral part of helping you grow.

Online, they'll be one of your biggest champions, communicating with others about what you do and helping you connect with more clients.

Regarding your communication at this point, you're more than likely going to rely solely on quick emails, Facebook or Skype messages. I do however suggest having a weekly phone catch up.

Think of it as your 'staff meeting'. You sit around your virtual table, and all discuss where you're at and what needs doing.

Always remember, that although your VA may be working autonomously, they'd still love to hear from you occasionally, even if it's just to say hi. I love when my clients give me a quick call to see all is well in my world and to share their wins (or sometimes to have a shoulder to lean on).

You see, as your VA relationship progresses, you'll have your communication down pact, and your VA will become more than an admin assistant. You'll find them to be more like a business partner who will always have your back.

A Great VA Will Know How to Communicate

I'll never put all the onus on a business owner to know how to communicate with a VA.

A VA is a business owner who has chosen to leave the corporate world (usually) to run their own business.

A skilled VA will be an outstanding communicator. They need to be. They work in the virtual space. It's an essential element of the VA role to be able to relate to clients and guide them into how the working relationship should go.

And please, never be scared to talk to your VA. If they're making errors, point them out (nicely of course), or they won't know. If they're doing a great job, tell them. If you don't think it's working, communicate this so you can find solutions.

To sum up, here's how to effectively communicate with your VA:

Find a VA who 'gets' you, responds how you like and matches your personality

Ask your VA about their preferred method of communication and make sure it matches yours

Be clear and concise (and patient in the 'dating' stages).

Make sure you're available to your VA (I've heard of many VAs having secret 'Bat Phone' access to their clients)

Trust that your VA may eventually read your mind and do things before you've even thought of it.

What would I know about communication?

Since 2009, I've been running my own VA and copywriting business, A Virtual Copywriting Monstar. Learning early on in business how to communicate with clients (I did tell one my crystal ball was broken), I soon learnt that this was truly the key to a successful working relationship. Having a passion for communicating in writing, I studied copywriting and now spend most of my days creating copy for numerous business owners who are struggling to communicate their message to the online world.

******

Recruitment

We've mentioned you need people, but you also need good systems to ensure you are finding the right people for the right tasks and supporting them to work to their best level. There are a number of options available to you when it comes to finding support. For example you may find hiring staff is more suitable for you. Alternatively you might prefer virtual staff, offshore contractors or onshore contractors. Let's have a look at some of these.

There are a few factors you should consider when weighing up whether to have employed staff or contractors (or both). If you're thinking of staff, ask yourself:

- Can I offer them regular, reliable work?
- Can I ensure they can access benefits such as sick leave, annual leave, WorkCover and superannuation?
- Can I afford to maintain their equipment, software, etc.?

In my experience, I've found that it's more than just the legalities and logistics of contractor versus staff that play a role in the decision-making process. The benefits are just as important.

Having a contractor who is also a business owner means that they understand what it's like to be running the show, having all of the responsibility and risk but also being able to create something that is truly unique.

Because they are also growing a business, they can share experiences, ideas and processes that they've found useful. They need to network for their own business and inadvertently end up networking for you too – seeing opportunities and potential partnerships and sending them your way. I call them 'opportunity radars'.

Fellow business owners also have to outsource (I only work with those who practice what they preach), and as such, they can respect how challenging it is to let go of pieces of your 'baby' and leave them in someone else's hands.

Onshore versus Offshore

There are great resources around which help you find not only onshore but also offshore VAs. The resources in Australia helping you find offshore support are usually looking at virtual staff. They often work for you full time or for a significant number of hours per month and at a very low rate. They have specific processes to follow and are hired through your Australian based contact.

You can also find plenty of independent offshore contractors in pretty much any country.

What I've found is that countries like the Philippines and India have the lowest hourly rate. Other places like the UK, Europe and the USA can be similar in cost to Australia but definitely vary across the board. What is consistent is that each country definitely has it's own business culture and style for getting things done. So working out which style works best for you and taking into account where your target market resides is important when determining the location of your support team.

The key benefits I've found for the cheaper offshore option is that yes, it's cheaper, but also they can be really great with getting those repetitive tasks done that you don't want to allocate a big budget to. I've heard of some great stories where people are getting wonderful admin support or even tech, social media or design support via this option. On the flip side I've heard of some serious time-wasters and have experienced some of those myself where the work quality is terrible and the communication is a battle of wits.

My view is that the onshore (Australian) based VAs have some extra value they can bring to the table. And this is important because they definitely cost more. Australian VAs will be able to communicate and connect really well with your Australian-based audience (if your audience is here) because they live the Australian life. They know cultural nuances that are almost impossible to understand if you don't live here.

They are also self employed which means they understand how running a business feels. They have to have initiative and be proactive, they need to network and connect. These all benefit you too because they bring those skills into your business. If they aren't proactive they won't survive in business – so they won't sit back and wait for you to send through tasks, they'll work with you to achieve more.

That all being said – there's going to be good and bad in every country. But hopefully we can help you find the best fit for you.

Your work style, your audience and their location are factors which can help you work out who to work with, but you may also find it useful to consider which generation connects best with your audience and will help fill gaps you might have in terms of generation-specific connections.

The reason I mention this is because if you are targeting a younger demographic, you may find you need a 'Millenial' to help you work on that strategy and to bring insights. Likewise if you are targeting an audience who are within the Generation X era you may need someone from that era to help you out.

Recruitment FAQs

Do you need a specific business structure before you hire a contractor?

I've had business owners ask me if they need to have a specific business structure in place before they hire a contractor. For example, does it make a difference if you're a company vs a sole trader?

With my business knowledge (and remember that I'm not an accountant), if you have an ABN, you can hire a contractor and claim the expenses under your business. So, whether you're a sole trader, a company, or trading under a trust, it makes no difference.

Do you need to have all the software in place that a VA may need?

No, you don't! Chat to your VA before you purchase any new software to see:

a)   if they use it or would recommend using it, and

b)   if they would recommend other software programs that would suit your business.

For project management, your VA may already be using a good program that you can use too. They'll need to set you up with your account and show you how it works.

Honestly, there's only one thing you must have in place.

The one thing you MUST have in place before you hire a Virtual Assistant is your vision.

You need to know what you want to achieve and make smart goals. You can then work on them with your awesome new VA. With these, you'll be well equipped to grow your team and achieve more in your beautiful, wonderful business.

The aim of someone running a business is that they are a specialist in their zone of genius and they can provide outstanding service to their clients. Being an industry that has gained a lot of momentum in the last couple of years, the VA/VC Industry has a lot of new business owners who are building their skill levels and experience – so it's important to be clear about what sort of support and experience level you need.

Where do I find a VA?

Over the years I've seen many people jump onto Facebook and ask in a large business group: "I need a VA to help me with such and such ... can you recommend someone?" after which they get completely bombarded with recommendations and offers of support.

Having lots of options seems great, but without a filtering process, it can simply become another task for you to wade through when you're already incredibly busy.

Instead, what I recommend is submit a request for support to a reputable Virtual Business network like Virtually Yours. VAs who take their business seriously know that being a part of a community of their peers is valuable and they value ongoing learning and collaboration.

Those are the VAs I'd want to work with. Sites like Virtually Yours let their membership know that you're seeking help and what the details are that you've provided. The VAs with the right skills and availability will contact you for a chat to see if you're a good fit for each other.

When you submit your request for support, being as detailed as possible and also including any personal elements that you may feel are good filters is a good idea. For example, if you predominantly work out of hours, or you're always on the phone and the go, or you want someone with a great sense of humour.

These are just as useful as the points you'll make about the skills and service you require. When working with a contractor for your business, you need to have a good connection and be able to create a shared vision. The best business relationships come from really knowing who you work well with and how to share your vision.

You can always ask your peers if they can recommend a VA. However be mindful that the VA who partners well with one person, may not with another. We are all human beings, and different tasks and personalities can make a huge difference in the outcome. So, by all means, ask – but do your homework with those people too.

What does it cost?

I wish I could give you a definitive price for this, but with the services and outcomes so varied it would be impossible. However, there are some general rules that you can go by if it helps.

One of the important things you need to know before hiring a VA is what YOU are worth. Knowing your value allows you to weigh up the potential income lost from doing the job yourself versus having someone else do it for you.

The other thing is being really clear on what you want to achieve from outsourcing.

- Is it to save time – what is that worth to you?
- Is it to move forward on a project – what is that worth to you?
- Is it to get something done that you can't do yourself no matter how long you spend on it – what's that worth to you?

Having a clear vision for your business is important – when you outsource or make any purchase without a plan, you potentially throw money away, and you have no real way of measuring the success of the purchase.

Australian Virtual Assistants usually charge anywhere upwards of $30 per hour. This is generally the starting rate because once the math is done, $30 is the minimum they'd need to charge to make a profit.

Business expenses for VAs can add up. They need to have good Internet, computer, monitor and laptop, quality mobile phone, Internet and phone lines, stationery, desk and varied office equipment, marketing and software costs, networking, ongoing training, coaching and membership expenses – the list goes on. Once they factor these in, they don't walk away with much from their $30 per hour. Add to that the fact that the $30 needs to cover them across the year for sick or annual leave and, if possible, superannuation.

It's usually the basic administration that gets charged out at this rate. However, as anyone who has run a business knows, quality administrative support is worth its weight in gold, and as such, the more experience, skill and insight a VA has, the more they will charge for it.

Some Australian VAs charge $55 per hour or more for business administration. These VAs are the Online Business Managers of the VA world, and they bring so much more than just 'ad hoc admin support'.

Not all VAs charge per hour either. You can arrange outcome based packages (not commission) where they deliver certain outcomes per week or month for example, and you pay a set price. If the outcomes change, obviously the price needs to be reassessed.

This method of pricing is what most of us are used to seeing every single day. We don't buy our lunch based on how long it took to make – we pay for it based on the outcome. The price is set based on what is needed to make it, which includes all business elements such as having the shop, kitchen, staff, food, skills, marketing etc. It's not just about the cost of the food itself. It's everything behind it and the problem it solves – you're hungry, and you're out and about without access to your kitchen and food.

As mentioned earlier, Virtual Contractors include graphic designers, social media managers, bookkeepers and copywriters to name just a few. So, it's to be expected that these would all range in cost based on service type and skill level.

How can I build trust?

Once you work your way though concerns about people seeing what your business management looks like and how you're going to communicate with them, you may find yourself worrying about 'trust'. Trusting your contractor with IP (Intellectual Property) and trusting that they're doing what they said they would be doing.

Having documents in place which include confidentiality, IP protection and privacy policies, are very important for establishing a relationship built on trust. The agreement sets out what the agreed terms are so there is no confusion.

Trusting that the contractor will adhere by it and also work as they say they're going to may be assisted by quality screening and obtaining testimonials. One thing you quickly learn in business is that the 'know, like, trust' factor is huge. So getting to know the contractor through a few conversations (a skype chat is great if you can't meet F2F), determining that you like them and they align with your values and building trust based on those factors plus testimonials, is a good way to start.

However, you need to ensure that your agreements are clear and that the consequences of breaching them are also clear. Sometimes, business relationships that start with the best of intentions don't end well, so cover yourself.

Your Virtual Contractor should be able to provide an agreement which includes what the agreed services will be, the delivery methods, timelines, pricing, payment terms and of course, privacy and confidentiality statements.

This agreement supports both parties to clearly understand the proposed partnership and should be signed by both parties. Also, include a review date, so you remember to reassess the terms and services a few months down the track – you can never really tell if the scope will change or not.

Before outsourcing, it's wise to speak to an insurance broker about any insurances you should have in place. I don't think it's wise to rely on your contractors to have insurance – cover yourself, so you know what will happen if anything goes awry. Also, speak to your accountant about what sort of business structure will be the best for you as you grow your business. For example, you may find that a company structure will better suit you than a sole trader.

What if things go wrong?

Let's not kid ourselves – stuff can go wrong. Sometimes when all seems wonderful at the start, it somewhere somehow goes sour. It happens to the best of us. Doing your best to find the right VA and communicate well is all you can do. Sometimes it's just not meant to be.

Always remain professional and rational.

Just because your relationship with your contractor isn't working, doesn't automatically mean that they're a terrible business owner, nor does it mean that you are. Try to look at the bigger picture and avoid making assumptions. Sometimes things don't pan out because personalities don't meld well, circumstances change or even job perspective changes.

If you find things aren't working and you want to stop working with your VA then please:

- Change passwords
- Pay what you owe
- Refer to your agreement
- Seek legal help if required

It can be easy to want to vent to your social media audience when things go wrong in business but make sure you avoid letting it all out in public forums. The last thing you want from a failed business arrangement is a slander lawsuit or people wondering whether you'd publicly shame them if they were to work with you.

What if I need more VAs?

There's no limit on how big you can make your team. It's also good to work with people who are working in their zone of genius. So, it would be hard to find one VA who can do everything.

However, as many teams do, having a key person managing the other team members is a smart way to keep things on track and reduce how many people YOU have to manage. A VA who can manage your business for you (often referred to as an Online Business Manager or OBM) would have enough skills to do certain tasks for you and manage others who do other tasks. They end up being your right-hand-woman as such. You can have semi-regular team meetings but more regular meetings with your OBM.

I love working directly with each of my team members. I have six different people with different roles in my business. They each have really clear strengths, and I love working with them around those.

For example the first VA I worked with on a long term basis was Monique. She helped me write some copy and did some admin work for me too. I found that she was an amazing ear and shoulder to cry on and she really helped me through the tough days of running a business.

I then brought on Korryn who helps me with some techy stuff I don't want to do and also lines up my webinar and podcast guests.

Kym helps me with some data work when I need it and checking my writing for grammar and spelling errors. She has an eagle eye!

Kristen has helped me run Facebook campaigns which has been a real load off my shoulders as I really dislike the FB ad manager area.

And Hanna and her team answer my phones because if they didn't – no one would. They also guide those callers through steps to submit leads or join my network via my website.

Finally I have my accountant, Ben, who works the finances with me.

I personally love liaising with each and every one of them so I don't have an OBM who 'manages' them for me. We are a team and I love working with them.

Technology

You need to ensure you are using technology effectively to be more leveraged with your time and impact. Technology is ever-changing, and there are incredible solutions out there to help you streamline systems and automate repetitive tasks. On the flip side, technology can also be a total pain and needs to be managed by someone who has the right skills to do so. Also, there are still many areas of your business which cannot yet be completed through technology and sometimes you will need humans as gap-fillers when systems can't do what you need.

What software programs are there that help?

You may find that your selected VA is already using and recommending file sharing software, or if you have one you are already using you can see if your VA can access it too.

Some of the programs I've heard a lot about include Asana, Trello, Basecamp and Teamwork. All are useful for collaborating. If you google these words and nothing comes up – it means they don't exist anymore. That's life these days! Programs do come and go. Virtual Assistants generally stay on top of what the best programs are and can provide advice around this.

When working with virtual contractors, you pretty much need to embrace the cloud. Your bookkeeping will need to be cloud-based if you use a virtual bookkeeper, your CRM and newsletter programs will need to be cloud-based and you'll need something like Dropbox to share files easily. Gsuite is currently a great option for file sharing and collaboration too.

Depending on what sort of business you're running you may need a website and someone to help you either create or manage it. You may also find you need to embrace social media platforms such as Facebook, LinkedIn or Twitter – depending on where your clients tend to 'hang out'.

All of this is in the cloud, and the beauty of that is that your team can all work on your business from their locations.

Your everyday email will no doubt be used a lot. There are even task management programs which pull from your emails to keep track of what you are doing. If you are working with a team, transparency helps avoid communication issues and time waste.

Here are some programs which you may want to explore:

Project Management

- Asana – asana.com
- Avaza – avaza.com
- Monday – monday.com
- Slack – slack.com
- Trello – trello.com

CRMs

- Active Campaign (includes eNewsletters) – activecampaign.com
- AgileCRM – agilecrm.com
- Capsule – capsulecrm.com
- Dubsado – dubsado.com
- Ontraport (includes eNewsletters) – ontraport.com
- Pipedrive – pipedrive.com
- Zoho – zoho.com

Bookkeeping/Invoicing

- Freshbooks – freshbooks.com
- Quickbooks - quickbooks.intuit.com/au
- Wave – waveapps.com
- Xero – xero.com/au

Timekeeping

- Get Harvest – getharvest.com
- Timecamp – timecamp.com
- Toggl -toggle.com
- Tsheets – tsheets.com

File Sharing

- Dropbox – dropbox.com
- Google Drive - google.com/drive/
- We Transfer – wetransfer.com

eNewsletters

- ConvertKit – convertkit.com
- GetResponse – getresponse.com
- MailChimp – mailchimp.com
- MailerLite – mailerlite.com

Social Media Scheduling

- Buffer – buffer.com
- Hootsuite – hootsuite.com
- Later – later.com
- Planoly – for Instagram – planoly.com

Password Security

- 1password – 1password.com
- LastPass – lastpass.com

Leadership

This ingredient is incredibly important. Teams simply can't function without the right leadership. Leadership comes down to the clarity of direction, understanding of yourself, your skills and your weaknesses, understanding of your team skills and weaknesses, and a huge dose of communication skills.

This is your boat; you need to guide it. Leadership means allowing your team to shine in the areas they are passionate and excited about. It means focusing on what you need to do and getting it done. Lead by example. Appreciate the contributions of others and always communicate the desired destination.

Leadership FAQs

How do we stay on track and inspired?

Shared visions, shared goals and great communication are all really important for staying on track and remaining inspired. When outsourcing for extended periods this becomes important for both parties. There's nothing harder than working on a business that doesn't inspire and invigorate you! Working towards shared goals and using the right software to stay on track should be part of your business strategy, as would regular catch ups on the phone or a program like Skype.

When you communicate your goals and visions to your contractors, you allow them to see what drives you. They also become more aware of relevant opportunities that would be good for you, that appear in front of them.

When your team feel like they're all valued and part of a mission, they work better. It's human nature.

It's worth mentioning that when you negotiate price and lowball your contractors, they're not going to feel very connected and inspired by you. The second you start doing this you're saying that you don't value what they do. As human nature does, this results in your contractor feeling pretty much the same way about you, and you may find that after the glow wears off, you haven't got much drive and inspiration left to keep things moving forward.

Same goes for feedback. Giving constructive feedback when appropriate is really helpful and giving positive feedback is always going to give your team a buzz – so don't hold back on that good stuff!

Ensure that you are both always on the same track. You both need to actively communicate so setting up regular meetings will be very helpful. In these meetings, you can look at what's working well, what's not, and suggested changes. (We have a Lead & Manage Template to help with this).

Keep exploring ways you can help each other work towards your business goals. Have fun and enjoy the business ride!

What if I want to have a holiday?

This is another benefit of outsourcing and having a VA who can be your OBM. With processes set up correctly, you should be able to take a break and leave things in their capable hands. Everyone needs holidays, so to think that you couldn't possibly and that your business would fall over without you, is pretty crazy.

You need to set things up so that current clients know what services they can or can't access while you are away, and so that new enquiries are responded to promptly by your VA and followed up on your return.

A perk of running a Virtual type of business is that you or your VA could technically work from anywhere. However, spending hard earned money on flights, accommodation and experiences is less tempting when you have to take your work with you. Just go all 'Elsa from Frozen' and let it go!

On the flip side, having a VA means that if something does go wrong or the most amazing opportunity in the world pops up while you are away, they can still usually get in contact with you, so you don't miss out. Unless your VA has the skills to manage all situations that may arise while you are away I don't recommend going off the grid for too long.

Your emails can be responded to in different ways. They can either have an autoresponder set up within your hosting account to let people know you are away. Or you can have them go to your CRM and be either managed by your VA or responded to according to workflows and the type of email they are. VAs often access clients' emails through accounts like Gmail and can respond and manage them for you either just while you are away, or even throughout the year.

If your VA works with you throughout the year they would normally be on top of your various projects and tasks anyway, so overseeing these while you are away shouldn't be a big change.

What if the VA gets sick or takes a holiday?

If your VA gets sick, a contingency plan needs to be implemented. That's why having those contingencies is so important. Even a bout of the flu can knock someone out for a couple of weeks which could have a significant effect on your business if you and your VA don't have a back-up plan.

With the right sort of planning and communication, you can keep things running if your VA does happen to fall sick for a short while. Your contingencies should look at what should happen if your VA is sick for a day or two, sick for more than a week to two weeks or sick for longer.

You'd be able to plan things more easily if the VA were going to be away for those same periods, but that's simply because you would be given prior warning. What's the plan if, without warning, your VA becomes unable to support you.

Some VAs will have other VAs who can step up and replace them during these periods. They may have a team of VAs or may have another VA business they work closely with. Discussing in advance what this would look like in implementation is important.

Having processes and procedures clearly outlined and accessible for times like this is vital too. The VAs who are a part of the contingency must know how to access these P&Ps when the time comes. Limited access to certain password protected files can be set up using programs like LastPass or 1password.

Working with a VA who has a team behind them can be more expensive but these situations make it worthwhile because the team members can step up and fill gaps as needed.

Virtual Insights by Sonya Stattmann

Success Strategist for Women in Service Businesses

sonyastattmann.com

I have been a business coach and mentor for 20 years. It has been an amazing journey and in that time I have learned a lot about what it takes to succeed in business. Currently, I specialise in helping women in service businesses, specifically: coaches, consultants, wellness practitioners and service professionals like graphic designers or marketers. I come from a very different approach to building a business that is designed to help women grow their business in a way that brings them more joy, fulfillment and financial freedom.

Having worked personally with thousands of women and observed many more, one of the most common issues I see for women in business is burnout! So many of the people you think are succeeding on social media or in the limelight are literally exhausted behind the scenes. I believe we have to be more honest about our experiences in business so we can find a path to more sustainable success.

Part of the path to having a successful business is knowing when and where to delegate. It is impossible to do it all yourself, and one of the things that leads to burnout is continuing to DIY long after you should have hired some help. Over the years, I have hired lots of VAs, experts and assistants to help me grow my business.

I have had both local VAs when I lived in the USA and Australia, and offshore VAs in places like the Philippines. I have used them for everything from admin to marketing. Currently I have a lovely VA in the Philippines. She catches everything for me that doesn't require my personal expertise or creativity. She helps with my social media posts, updates my website, prepares my sales calls and helps me keep track of each and every client in my program. She saves me hours of time each week and I don't know what I would do without her.

I am a fan of hiring VAs and I teach my clients when and where to do it. The timing and sequence of hiring a support team makes a huge difference to your success or struggle. You don't want to hire them too early or too late. Sometimes business owners think they need to hire a VA because they are personally overwhelmed and trying to do too much. If you are overwhelmed and not sure what you should be focusing on in your business, a VA is not the best person to help. This is where you need to hire a business coach or mentor who can help you look at your business and streamline it.

When women start working with me, I cut out 80% or more of what they are doing in their business, because it is a waste of time. Most people are doing things that produce no return on their effort. Paying someone else to handle the tasks that produce no return for your business is not the best move. You need a streamlined business and a solid foundation first!

Once your business is solid and profitable, and you are running it efficiently, that is the best time to focus on growth. This is where a VA is invaluable. You can start getting off your plate all the little tasks that don't require your expertise and creativity, so you can take on more work in your genius zone.

I started with delegating tech. Tech is not my genius zone and it stresses me out. I also think delegating repetitious tasks is a good first step. As you get comfortable with your VA, you can start delegating more and more. Now, I start doing something and think, "I don't need to be doing this" and I send a note to my VA to do it for me. It leaves me to focus on teaching, coaching and sales which are my genius areas.

Finding the right VA is about personal choice and what you need in your business. I highly recommend doing your due diligence. Trusting parts of your business to others is a big step and you want someone you align with and know you can trust. I also would recommend you have nailed down your own systems and business structures before you delegate them to someone else. I see a VA as an extension of me, like another arm, not as a replacement for my knowledge and expertise in my business. I have to continue to be at the helm of my ship!

4 STEPS TO BUILD YOUR TEAM

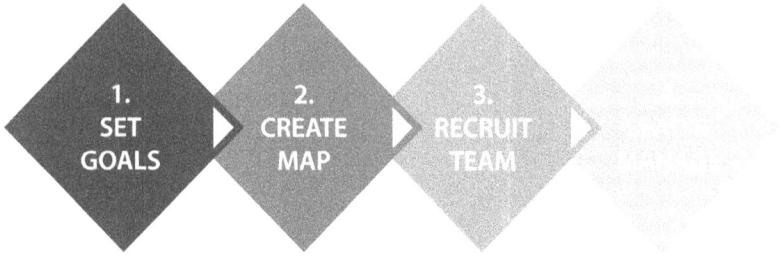

Step 1: Set Goals

Having a plan is the first step. If you aren't sure why you want a VA or what you want to achieve from it, you should have a discovery session with a VA who has lots of business experience or a business coach first.

Once you have a plan, you'll be able to communicate that plan clearly to your contractors and start working towards the end goals together. Being able to outline a plan will help guide all of your processes moving forward and help you assess what is working well and what isn't.

Let's explore where you're at in your business at the moment. Take a piece of paper mark out four columns. Call the first column 'I'm here now'.

In this column, make a list of points of where you are in your business right now. How many hours are you working? How satisfied are you with your life balance? What have you achieved to date? What are you making financially?

In the second column, I want you to write down where you want to be and when beside each of the points from column 1.

For example, if you had 'I'm working 40 hours per week' in column 1, I want you to state in column 2 how many hours you want to be working – what you're striving towards.

Column 3 should be labelled 'Current issues that need to be addressed'. Here you write down what the issues are that need to be addressed so you can get from column 1, to column 2.

In column 4 you need to write down what you think possible solutions to those issues are. We call that column 'potential solutions' – clever huh?

Here's an example for you.

I'm here now

- I'm working 40 hours per week.

I want to be here

- I'm working 20 hours per week

Current issues that need to be addressed

- I spend a lot of time on bookkeeping and social media
- I'm working 1:1 instead of 1:many
- I'm working while my kids are underfoot.

Proposed solutions

- Get a bookkeeper on board
- Get a social media VA on board
- Work with someone to implemement my signature system educate model as a group program
- Co-working space with childcare

Have a good look at the potential solutions and see what you think will work and what may not (or may need to be postponed for now). Highlight the stuff you want to turn into action items.

Once you get all of this out of your head, it's a good idea to ensure your closest stakeholders are on board. By that, I mean your family (partner and kids)! Make sure they know what you're trying to achieve and what steps you want to take to achieve them. You need to have support and also accountability to move forward in your business. And often, those goals you've set will benefit the family so they'll be more likely to support you if they can see what it is you're aiming for.

If you struggle to fill out the spreadsheet, it may be worth sitting down with a peer, best friend, coach or mentor to help. You don't have to do this alone!

Step 2: Map

Once you've set out your goals, you need to start mapping out an action plan. To do this, you need to break down the action items into tasks. This is because we want to know the following:

- How will you achieve your goals?
- Who will be involved and in what capacity?
- How will you measure success?

Let's use an action item as an example. Let's say that one of your action items was 'Get a social media VA on board'. The task that you wanted to achieve is 'set up and implement a social media strategy'. To do this, you need a Social Media VA. What are your expectations of that person? What are your goals?

For example:

Tasks

- Create and implement a social media strategy

Role

- Social media VA

Expectations

- Posting daily to my Facebook page with content sourced from me, my newsletter or preferred partners.

Goals

- Increase interaction through social media and increase the number of followers who sign up to the newsletter.
- Assess impact each month and look at what types of posts get the best result

Do this for each of the action items so you have a clear list of what you want to achieve and who will be working on these.

Make sure you are clear on what the goal is for you because the task, role and expectation can be approached differently depending on that important reason WHY.

Step 3: Recruit

Here's the fun bit! Or the scary bit. Take your pick.

For the action items needing external support, we explore recruitment. In this book, we look at recruiting contractors (or Virtual Assistants).

If you're a little worried about outsourcing to a Virtual Assistant, then you're not alone. Most business owners worry that they need to have all their ducks in a row before they hire a contractor.

Although this is a lovely idea, let's keep this real. Not many of us (business owners) have all our ducks in a row

– there's always a rogue little one ducking things up. And if you're too busy focusing on the rogue duck, the regular ducks will start acting up too, and all your ducks can go wild.

Businesses, especially online businesses, are always evolving. Your ducks will rarely line up for more than a second at a time.

And that's ok.

You don't need your ducks to be lined up before you get help from a Virtual Assistant

A Virtual Assistant should be able to help you get things moving along, more systemised and more effective. You DON'T need to have everything sorted before you hire a VA.

The ABC of Recruitment

Although there are many awesome VAs out there who specialise in a range of areas, the following questions will help you use the Virtually Yours VA Request Form to filter out those who don't meet your requirements and leave you with some great choices to assist you with your business needs. Always remember that our VAs are INDEPENDENT CONTRACTORS. They are not staff. They set their rates and you must sign an agreement before commencement.

Below is my process for finding a VA.

Process for Finding a VA

Good filtering comes from asking the right questions – fill in the responses here, to save time before filling in the online form.

ASK ...

Where do you want to take your business? What is the dream?

_____

_____

_____

List the jobs you know you want your VA to perform now.

This gives the VA an insight into what you need right away, and allows them to quote accordingly.

_____

_____

_____

List the jobs you may want your VA to perform into the future.

This gives the VA insight into future requirements and lets them decide whether this is work they can assist you with or not.

_____

_____

_____

State the amount of time you believe the jobs you have now will take.

Remember that the VA will quote based on the time they think it will take, but this gives them an estimate to work from. Be realistic!

_____

_____

_____

Is this an ongoing opportunity, or a once off task?

It is good to state this very clearly so the VA can respond accordingly.

_____

_____

_____

What mode of communication do you best work with?

Some people are better at phone, some at email – how do you communicate most/best?

_____

_____

_____

State whether the VA will need to come to your work premises, or not throughout the tenure.

Generally VAs work virtually, however some may be happy to attend meetings or events. Making this clear filters out those who work virtually only.

_____

_____

_____

Do you have a preference for VA availability times?

You may need a VA who is available from 9am to 5pm, or this may not matter in your type of work. Again, this is a good filtering process for VAs to respond to.

_____

_____

_____

Who is your target market?

_____

_____

_____

Fill in the form at

https://www.virtuallyyours.com.au/submit-a-job-request/

Using the information above, fill in the online form with as much detail as you can. This will ensure that only relevant responses are received.

Believe – Take a Leap of Faith

Here are some questions to ask to help you review your responses received.

- Did the VA respond to all of your requests about tasks required, future requirements, times allocated, pricing and any other requirements within your submission?
- Did the VA tell you why they would be the best person for the tasks/jobs you need?
- Was the VA prompt and professional in their response?
- Does the VA have a clear onboarding process for you to follow?

As you hear from VAs, take note of how their email or call made you feel. Did you get good vibes from reading their introduction or chatting to them?

I suggest doing the following:

1. Jot down their name, their contact details and the skill set they've outlined

2. As you hear from VAs highlight any differences, you see

3. Feel free to stalk their online business profiles to check out who they are

In an online world, I get that it's hard to trust. I'm a big believer that the fastest way to trust is to talk face to face. I highly suggest that once you've shortlisted, you pick up the phone to talk to the VAs. Use a program like Skype so you can see them.

- Do they present themselves well in person?
- Do they seem nervous? If yes, why?
- Do they answer your questions?
- Did they make you feel relieved that they'll do a great job?

Commence

You can start with one or two tasks as a trial, or a 1-3 month trial period to make sure you're a good fit.

As with any business venture with a contractor, you should make sure you have a signed agreement in place. This covers you, your business and the VA. It's vital in case anything happens (i.e. discrepancy with invoices/payments) that you have it all in writing.

Outline what the role involves, so you're both clear.

Many VAs will have a confidentiality agreement that you can both sign (or you can have one) that covers the VA not disclosing any information about your business to a third party etc.

Outline the agreed pricing, whether it's a package or an hourly rate with set hours.

If you need certain deliverables/KPIs (i.e. due dates for a blog etc.) make sure you have this in writing too.

Start with small tasks and get to know each other.

Share your goals and challenges with your VA so they know how they can best support you. Set KPIs for the business.

Focus on communication.

Understand that what may be obvious to you is not always going to be obvious to your team members. You know your business so well you may take that knowledge for granted. Be patient and give this time.

Step 4: Lead & Manage

Leading your team

Having one VA or a team of VAs has the amazing benefit of saving you time and allowing you to focus on what you do best. We all know this. But what we also need to realise is that when you have a team – of one, two or more, you will need to step up and lead them.

Leading people does not mean telling them how to work, or micromanaging. Leading means ensuring you're all on the same page, heading for the same goals and outcomes. Leading means showing up and being an example of how you want your business to run. It means communicating what you need, what you want to achieve and how you envisage getting there.

The best partnerships allow each contributor to shine in their area of expertise. Allow the copywriter to write. Allow the marketer to market. But ensure that they know what you're trying to achieve and by when. And where possible, allow them to be part of a team and be aware of what each of the cogs in your machine is doing.

When you have a team the following elements are vital:

- Communication
- Respecting skills
- Respecting each other's understanding of the goal and always ensuring gaps are filled
- Leading by example
- Never assuming.

Too often I hear business owners saying that they 'assumed something would be happening' or 'assumed it was going to be done a particular way' – and it wasn't. We all know about assumptions. They aren't a smart business habit to have.

If you want to save time and make things work for you, you need to clarify and confirm. Much like spending less money and hoping to achieve the same outcome, not spending the small effort to clarify and confirm while hoping to streamline and leverage doesn't work out.

Your VA team can help you streamline, but when it comes to leading and managing a team, you can't cut corners. Always consider how you'd feel if you were on a team and you weren't being guided appropriately. You bring amazing skills to the table but aren't being told how they need to be applied, what the priorities are, what the rest of the team are working on and what the end goal is. It makes it frustrating and uninspiring.

The best teams are excited, passionate and inspired. If you want to run a successful business, you need to step up and lead in such a way that allows for this to happen.

Lead & Manage Communication Worksheet

You can use this (next page) regularly to stay on track with your team members.

Having a plan on how you lead and manage your contractors is important, just because they work virtually doesn't mean that it's a one way street with directives coming from you as a client. Having regular communication and feedback with your team members will help strengthen your team and your business.

TEAM MEETINGS

Preferred communication method

Email - Phone - Video Call - Instant Messenger

Team meeting frequency

Weekly - Fortnightly - Monthly - Adhoc

Team Member KPIs:

(The key deliverables that were agreed at the commencement of your engagement with your Virtual Contractor)

_____

_____

_____

Feedback Items for Team:

(Working with outsource providers work well when there are communication and feedback about their work - do you have feedback you'd like to give your team?)

_____

_____

_____

What's working well

(Celebrate the wins and what is working well with the engagement and work being produced. Ask the same of your team member - what do they see is working well.)

_____

_____

_____

_____

_____

What needs improvement?

(Constructive feedback on what needs improvement is an integral part of building a strong trust with your team. Also ask the same question to your team member, what do they see as areas that can be improved?)

_____

_____

_____

Proposed solutions / ideas

(This is from your perspective and then ask the question of your virtual contractor.)

_____

_____

_____

BY WHOM	DUE BY	TO DO LIST / ACTION ITEMS

SPEAK UP AND LET'S SHINE TOGETHER.

Virtual Insights by Annemarie Cross

The Podcasting Queen | Podcasting With Purpose

www.podcastingwithpurpose.com

My business is Podcasting With Purpose, helping Change Makers go from Invisible to Influential (and Profitable) with a Podcast.

I've been in business for over two decades (Personal Branding & Coaching in the career industry), later working with entrepreneurs helping them get noticed, hired and paid what they're worth, and now leveraging my ten plus years in podcasting in my business Podcasting With Purpose.

I began using an Onshore VA who helped me with uploading articles and blog posts to my website, sending off my newsletter and other core admin tasks, which was an incredible help. Sadly, she handed in her resignation several months in, as she had been reading the articles (as she uploaded them) and realised she wasn't living her purpose as a VA and therefore decided to change her career path.

Through recommendations I soon found another VA - who was working with a number of other businesses, so I knew she was passionate about her business. She not only took over my admin functions, but also my customer service and sales functions. I systematized my entire enquiry and sales process, diverted my phone/messages to her and she handled it all. I never met her, however she lived down the road from me.

As my business started evolving to work with entrepreneurs, I slowly wound down my career consultancy, however as I built up my personal branding and positioning with entrepreneurs I started outsourcing admin work to Offshore staff, including

- Social media scheduling
- Article posting
- Newsletter set up and sending out to my database and general administrative functions

Fast forward to today and I have:

- An Online Business Manager who supports me in all of my tech and business management. She's onshore and handles customer service, website, ecommerce technology and everything in between.
- Two Offshore VAs who work with me personally for my social media scheduling, podcast scheduling, graphic creation and my client work etc
- Other virtual team who are specialised in audio, graphic design, web design, etc who I will use project by project

I recommend that you document and systematise everything. Step by step outlines, along with video snippets to help train and onboard your team. Keep it in a place that is easily accessible by all parties and be willing to be patient as you are onboarding new team members.

Set guidelines and expectations on what is required so everyone knows exactly what they are doing and correctly.

My team are an extension of me and just because they aren't in my office, or only working a certain amount of hours, they are integral so treat people as you would like to be treated, with respect.

If there is a mix up or mistake - the buck stops with me as the leader of my business. And, it means I need to explain myself better so my team can be empowered to do their jobs properly.

My top tips for anyone wanting to outsource:

- Be totally clear on your requirements and expectations. VAs are wonderful, BUT they can't read your mind NOR can they work to your expectations if you haven't clearly outlined what you need.
- Document, document, document every process. Systemization is key and is important if you want to empower your team members to be able to do their jobs with you having to micromanage. In fact, if you're micromanaging it either means you've (a) hired the wrong person for the role (b) you haven't been clear in your requirements (c) you haven't got a clear process

in place they can follow, or maybe a combination of those. Or (d) you're an a-hole, who probably shouldn't be working with anyone and your VA may just end up firing you!

- Leverage tools to help you manage your team, such as Google Docs, Dropbox, Trello etc
- Be the type of leader that empowers your team to make suggestions of doing things better. If they can see a better way, faster way, etc of doing something, create a space where they can step forward confidently and share the idea.
- Treat your team with respect. How you treat your team members is a direct reflection of who you are. And HOW they perform is also a direct reflection of the person and leader you are.

IN CONCLUSION

RUNNING A BUSINESS IS UNIQUE. It's challenging. It's a constant learning curve. But you don't need to do it alone. And really, you shouldn't do it alone.

When you allow others to support you, you'll find your opportunities, creativity and reach all grow too. Once you start, you'll never go back.

Yes, you may need to kiss a few frogs before you find your perfect match, but if you learn from each experience, it can only be a good thing.

Ironically it took me a long time to get regular support for my business. I tapped into resources here and there for some years, never finding the exact right fit for me. For me, there was the interesting added factor that I run services for VAs, so hiring them to see how I do that did feel a little odd at first. Especially when my systems weren't well set up.

But over the years I've grown my team and now have not only a broad scope of skills available to me, but I have a group of women who support me, inspire me, find opportunities for me and pick me up when I'm feeling down. They make me laugh long and hard. They let me cry – but only briefly. They've allowed me to guide them in their businesses too so we can all grow together. They support each other too. It's wonderful.

My VA team are not expensive. They are priceless. As the cost of their support increases, so does my business success.

If you are currently doing it all yourself, please stop. Do the worksheets in this book and start speaking to VAs who can bring value to your business. Value beyond just the tasks. The camaraderie, the insights, the ideas. And if you do it right, the friendships.

Virtual Insights by Danielle Price

Founder, She Will Shine

shewillshine.com.au

I'm the Founder of She Will Shine, a community to support and connect women entrepreneurs around the country. With over 10 years small business experience I have discovered first-hand that it's who you surround yourself with that determines how you feel about your business, your life and yourself. And that's where She Will Shine thrives. We help women working alone to say goodbye to isolation and help them connect with genuine women who understand the challenges they face each day.

Over the years I have had VAs assist me with event planning, content formatting on my website and social media. I have always sourced my VAs onshore here in Australia as I have felt it would be easier communication and time wise.

I have always found my VAs either from existing connections or from trusted sources such as Virtually Yours. For this reason I already have a huge amount of trust in their ability and what they will be able to help me and my business achieve. Allowing extra time in the initial on-boarding process has always been beneficial to ensure both parties involved understand the process and outcomes required.

My top tips for anyone wanting to outsource? Start with the easy to hand over jobs. As these jobs progress and you feel more comfortable, increase the VAs responsibility so that your time is spent focusing on the bigger picture for your business.

ACKNOWLEDGEMENTS

WRITING A BOOK is a daunting task at the best of times but when you have as much support around you as I do, it suddenly becomes a very real thing and you suddenly find yourself holding onto an actual, real, with words and everything, book.

This is my third book. But the audience for this book is different to that of my other two. So I needed some extra cheering on by my super amazing friends and peers so that I'd get it over the line.

Firstly to Renee Hasseldine who has shown me that I have something of value to share and how easy it can be to share it and for writing my wonderful Foreword.

To Monique for never batting an eyelid when called upon to read through my pages and pages of content and waving her wand over it and of course for her amazing communications contribution to this book.

To Evelyne for always jumping in to make everything look good from start to finish!

To my biz peeps, Korryn and Kym for checking over my content and for your unwavering support and constant laughs.

To my husband who without question believes that I can do whatever I set my mind to. To my daughters Ruby and Ella, for making sure I need to keep earning money because they so eagerly spend it (and for actually reading the business books I write! Super cute!)

And to Hannah for always being my most supportive, crazy, awesome friend. Love ya guts.

Special thank you must also go to the amazing, inspiring business women and men who contributed their Outsourcing Insights to this book. Kate Toon – SEO and Copywriting royalty; Sonya Stattmann – passionate and powerful business coach; Annemarie Cross – the podcasting queen; Hannah Naylor – eco warrior extraordinaire; Jenny De Lacy – visibility video superstar, Emily Chadbourne – the antidote to the saber tooth tiger, Caroline Kropack – sweet tooth powerhouse, Danielle Price – the Shiniest One and Michael Griffith – the referral wizard – you are all absolutely amazing and to have you involved in this book absolutely makes my heart sing.

THANK YOU!

WHO IS ROSIE SHILO?

THERE ARE NOW NEARLY one million people running a home-based business in Australia. Working from home can offer flexibility and convenience and is a feasible option for many mothers looking for that work/life balance.

So, it's not big news that the Virtual Assistant is booming. But without industry pioneers and advocates, businesses of Australia would not know about the quality of VAs right here on Australian shores.

Virtually Yours is one of the pioneer Virtual Assistant businesses in Australia.

Back in 2004, before it was 'trendy', Rosie Shilo started Virtually Yours. Working as a nanny, Rosie saw the need for mothers to be able to work from home to have time with their children.

So years before having her children, Rosie, using her background knowledge of administration, decided to go it alone. Starting out working for a handful of clients, she found herself needing to constantly explain to business owners about working 'virtually'.

Many business owners could not grasp the Virtual Assistant concept.

After all, didn't a 'Secretary' need to sit outside of your office and answer your phone, open your mail, fetch your coffee...But tirelessly, Rosie pushed on, networking in local business groups and spreading the word about Virtual Assistants.

As the industry grew, so did Rosie's popularity. Being known as the 'mother duck', VAs from across Australia, started approaching Rosie to ask for advice. Seeing the need for these emerging Virtual Assistants to feel like they belong, Rosie began her network.

Virtually Yours has now grown to a thriving Virtual Assistant network here in Australia, with over 160 members from across Australia.

For Virtual Assistants, Rosie provides:

- An online forum where they can connect, bounce ideas around and understand that although they work virtually, they are not alone
- Access to jobleads
- The opportunity for mentoring to grow their own Virtual Assistant business, with all the how to's and shortcuts that Rosie has learnt on her journey

For Australian Businesses, Rosie provides:

- Education (in the form of presentations/networking) about how to work with a Virtual Assistant, the costs involved and how to weigh up whether they should use a Virtual Assistant

- Access to a network of Australian Virtual Assistants where they can place a joblead for a project (short or long term) to find their perfect Virtual Assistant – for free

This passionate woman who has been described many times as 'awesome' is a true asset to the Virtual Assistant industry, and her desire to see the industry grow and develop shines through in everything she does.

APPENDIX 1

Tasks VAs can help you with

A Virtual Assistant is someone who can assist you with business related tasks as a contractor. They work offsite and, when you hire a self-employed VA, they understand what it means to run a business.

So, you can work on what you want to work on, while the LSTs (Life Sapping Tasks) are handled by someone else!'

Administration

- Internet research
- Minute taking (onsite or virtual)
- Reminder services
- Reporting
- Sourcing quotes
- Print management

Audio & video

- Editing videos / podcasts
- Editing audio files
- Recording audios
- Uploading audios / podcasts
- Uploading videos
- Audio Book publishing support

Author support

- eBook creation from existing documents
- eBook promotion
- Amazon management
- Book editing
- Publishing support

Customer services

- Answering website support tickets
- Answering website Chat enquiries
- Sending cards/gifts to clients
- Responding to email enquiries

Bookkeeping

- Bookkeeping data entry
- Invoicing
- Payment of accounts
- Debt collection

Databases

- Cleaning up, managing and updating databases
- CRM support
- Data entry

Diary management

- Appointment booking
- Booking travel, accommodation and flights
- Travel management

Documentation

- Business template creation
- File management (Dropbox, Google Drive, etc.)
- Formatting documents
- PDF conversion
- PDF creation
- Policy development and maintenance
- PowerPoint / Keynote presentations
- Preparing minutes
- Procedure development and maintenance

Email management

- MailChimp mail outs (emailers, newsletters)
- Setting up autoresponders
- Syncing calendars and making appointments
- Subscriber management

Events

- Event Straregies
- Conference registrations
- Setup of webinars
- Taking payments for events
- Webinar recording
- Booking speaking engagements
- Following up new contacts
- Event promotions
- Event follow-ups

Graphic design

- Branding / logo design and development
- Desktop publishing
- Photoshop and image editing
- Creating infographics
- Social media graphics
- Banners and signage
- Magazines
- Advertisements
- eBook and book covers

HR support and recruitment

- Real estate support
- Project management
- Mortgage broker support
- Team management
- Training

Marketing

- Blog posting
- Arranging promotions
- Arranging partnerships
- Marketing strategies
- Social media advertising
- Content Repurposing

Podcasting

- Podcast channel setup
- Podcast training
- Podcast management

Phones

- Outbound phone calls
- Reception services
- Lead follow up

Sales

- Lead generation
- Participate in forums online on your behalf
- Follow up contacts
- Reporting

SEO support

- Directory submissions
- Tag management
- Keyword setup
- Keyword research

Social media

- Social Media Strategies
- Creating and managing Facebook groups or Pages
- Managing and utilising Facebook Insights
- Creating and managing LinkedIn pages or groups

- Creating and managing Pinterest accounts
- Creating and managing Twitter accounts
- Creating and managing Youtube accounts
- Creating and managing Instagram accounts

Transcription

- Legal transcription
- Medical transcription
- Focus group transcription
- Interview transcription
- Lecture Transcription
- Transcription of video and audio files
- Typing up handwritten notes
- Dictation

Websites

- eBay listings
- Filter and respond to blog / website comments
- Updating online shops
- Updating websites of all kinds
- Uploading videos to YouTube, website or other programs
- Website creation and maintenance
- Website copywriting
- Landing pages
- Setting up opt-ins

- Social media Integration
- Website security
- CRM integration

Writing

- Blog writing
- Business tender writing
- Editing
- Proofreading
- Resume writing
- Writing of emailers
- Writing of newsletters
- Writing product descriptions
- Editing and proofreading blogs
- Editing and proofreading e-newsletters
- Writing press releases
- Guest blogging / management

As you can see, many services can be provided by Virtual Assistants. As with any industry, it's important to find a VA who suits your style and your business brand. Look for VAs who are constantly working on improving their skills and services and ask your VA if they outsource any of their business tasks - it's great if they do!

A self-employed Virtual Assistant, who has been Virtually Yours 'reference checked' or recommended through word of mouth is a great place to start when looking for a great VA.

If you have any questions, ask us!

Visit

virtuallyyours.com.au

to access all of my resources and contact details.

www.ingramcontent.com/pod-product-compliance
Lightning Source LLC
Chambersburg PA
CBHW071700210326
41597CB00017B/2264